The natural disaster Prepper's survival bible

Your Complete Guide to
Surviving Earthquakes,
Floods, Hurricanes, and More
(Before, During, and After)

Jeffery J. Gaskin

Table of contents

Part I: Preparing for the Storm

Chapter 1: Understanding the Threat Landscape—Knowing Your Enemy

Before we go into the details of stockpiling and home fortification, let's establish the framework for educated readiness. This chapter digs into the broad realm of natural catastrophes, preparing you to recognize possible risks in your own backyard and beyond.

Categories of Natural Disasters: A Rogue's Gallery of Fury
Mother Nature has a large arsenal of destructive powers at her disposal, each with its own distinct impact on the environment and necessitating specialized preparation tactics. Let's become familiar with some of the most prevalent natural catastrophe kinds.

Earthquakes: When tectonic plates move, waves of energy are unleashed, which may topple buildings, produce landslides, and destroy infrastructure across the area.

Floods: Rising water levels caused by excessive rains, overflowing rivers, or storm surges may flood large areas, interrupting transportation, poisoning water supplies, and presenting serious threats to life and property.

Hurricanes: These destructive tropical storms bring heavy rain, strong winds, and storm surges, which may cause devastation on both beaches and interior locations.

Tornadoes: These fiercely spinning columns of air rush over the country, smashing apart houses and destroying trees with their incredible force. While they are often isolated, their unpredictable nature makes them very deadly.

Wildfires: Uncontrolled fires fuelled by dry vegetation and high winds may quickly consume whole forests, cities, and even regions, endangering both natural ecosystems and human populations.

This is just a sampling of the many types of natural catastrophes. Other disasters, such as volcanic eruptions, tsunamis, and blizzards, might cause devastation depending on your location. Familiarizing yourself with the unique threats common in your area is critical for designing your preparation strategy.

Regional Risk Assessments: Map Your Vulnerability Zone
Understanding your local catastrophe environment is the foundation for successful preparation.

Historical Disaster Occurrences: Analyze previous occurrences in your location to determine the sorts of catastrophes that have occurred and their frequency. This information may be gathered from government organizations, weather services, and historical documents.
Risk Zones and Hazard Maps: Many locations include comprehensive maps that show areas prone to certain calamities such as floods, landslides, and wildfires. Familiarize yourself

with these maps to better understand your property's susceptibility.

Local Emergency Plans and Evacuation Routes: Knowing your community's official response plans and established evacuation routes will be very useful during a crisis. Familiarize yourself with the evacuation plans and practice them with your family.

Actively mapping your vulnerability zone gives you a significant edge when preparing for prospective attacks. Remember that information is power while dealing with natural calamities.

Assessing Your Home and Property: Identifying Weaknesses and Strengthening Defenses

Once you've identified the hazards you face, it's time to focus on your own house and property. Conduct a comprehensive examination to identify possible vulnerabilities and places that may be susceptible to certain calamities.

Structural integrity: Assess the strength of your structure, especially the roof, walls, and foundation. Are there any fissures or weaknesses that might exacerbate during an earthquake or strong winds?

Utilities and lifelines: Verify the security of electrical wiring, gas lines, and plumbing. Are they securely secured and shielded from possible damage?

Debris hazards: Look for loose things on your property, such as trees, branches, or outdoor furniture, that might become projectiles in strong winds or storms.

Evacuation routes: Plan clear and unimpeded exits from your house in case of an emergency. Ensure exits are clear and clutter-free. Designate a secure and accessible area for emergency supplies. This should be a safe place, free of possible threats such as water or falling debris.

By proactively identifying and resolving weaknesses, you may turn your house into a safe haven in the event of a crisis. Remember, even little changes may make a big impact in safeguarding your loved ones and property.

Beyond the Basics: Deep Dive into Specific Disasters

While this part offered a basic overview, more study into specific catastrophe types common in your area is strongly advised. This may involve:

Understanding the complexities of earthquake preparedness: Exploring earthquake-resistant building methods, retrofitting alternatives for existing houses, and securing furniture and appliances. Familiarize yourself with earthquake-resistant measures such as attaching bookcases to walls and anchoring water heaters to prevent them from tumbling.

Flood Mitigation Strategies: Investigating flood proofing methods for doors and windows, installing sump pumps and backflow prevention valves, and preparing sandbags for possible flooding disasters. Consider elevating electrical outlets and appliances in flood-prone regions to reduce damage.

Hurricane preparation checklists: Learn about hurricane shutters and impact-resistant windows, as well as how to secure unsecured outdoor objects such as grills and patio furniture and prepare your roof for strong winds. Trim tree branches around your home on a regular basis to avoid them becoming missiles in high winds.

Wildfire preparedness: Clear brush and combustible plants around your property to create defensible space, install fire-resistant roofing materials, and ensure firefighters have easy access to water supplies.

Create a Personal Vulnerability Profile
Beyond your home's physical weaknesses, think about your own personal requirements and situations. This includes:
Family members with specific needs: Do you have any elderly, handicapped, or small children in your home? Their special needs and requirements must be included in your preparation plan, such as obtaining medical supplies or devising evacuation procedures for persons with mobility issues.
Pets and livestock: Don't forget about your furry pals! Include pet food, cages, and leashes

in your emergency pack to ensure their safety, and locate pet-friendly shelters or evacuation routes as needed.

Dietary restrictions and allergies: If you or your family members have special dietary requirements or allergies, stock up on non-perishable food products and pharmaceuticals to guarantee their safety during a disaster. Access to transportation and communication: Evaluate your abilities to escape and communicate during a crisis. Do you have any other modes of transportation if the highways are blocked? Plan for backup communication options such as battery-powered radios or satellite phones in the event of a power loss.

Moving Forward: From Knowledge To Action
Understanding the hazards you face, analyzing your vulnerabilities, and adapting your preparation strategy are all critical steps toward limiting the effect of natural catastrophes. Remember that information is power, and proactive preparation may dramatically increase your chances of surviving the storm and emerging stronger on the other side

Chapter 2: Developing Your Preparation Mindset: From Fear to Fortitude

Facing the potential chaos of a natural catastrophe may elicit a variety of emotions, including dread, worry, and denial. However, in the face of uncertainty, adopting a proactive and prepared mentality is essential for successful disaster resilience. This chapter digs into the psychological foundations of readiness, helping you go from paralyzing dread to empowered action.

Overcoming Fear and Denial: Recognizing the Value of Proactive Preparation

Natural catastrophes may create feelings of vulnerability and anxiety. Images of rampaging floods, crumbling buildings, and fleeing people may be overwhelming, prompting denial or inaction. However, yielding to these emotions impedes our capacity to prepare properly.

Understanding fear: Fear is a normal human reaction to perceived dangers. It acts as a basic alarm system, warning us to avoid danger. However, unmanaged fear may immobilize us and prevent us from taking the essential precautions to reduce danger.

Confronting Denial: Denial is a psychological defensive strategy that permits us to temporarily avoid unpleasant facts. While it may provide temporary comfort, it prevents us from taking necessary precautionary measures before a calamity occurs.

shifting the paradigm: The trick is to reframe our perception. Instead of perceiving preparation as a difficult activity motivated by dread, we might reframe it as a powerful act of self-reliance and accountability. By adopting preventive measures, we gain control and reduce the potential effect of calamities on ourselves and our loved ones.

Developing A Proactive Mindset: Here are some techniques for developing a proactive and prepared mindset:

Education and Awareness: Knowledge is powerful. Learn about the unique hazards in your area, as well as the many kinds of disasters and their possible consequences. This information enables you to make educated judgments and plan efficiently.

Small Steps, Big Impact: Begin small. Don't overload yourself by attempting to complete everything at once. Begin with easy chores such as assembling a basic emergency pack or developing a family communication strategy. Gradually build on these tiny victories to generate a feeling of momentum and accomplishment.

Focus on the Positive: Framing preparation as a kind of self-care and safety for yourself and your loved ones may change the emotional narrative. Imagine the peace of mind and comfort that comes from knowing you've taken the essential precautions to secure their safety.

Prioritizing Needs and Resources: Setting Realistic Goals and Allocation of Budget
With the proactive mentality in place, it is time to turn intentions into tangible actions. This includes establishing realistic objectives,

prioritizing your needs, and allocating your resources wisely.

Needs assessment: The first step is to determine your individual demands and weaknesses. Consider your family's size, dietary limitations, medical requirements, and availability of resources. This requirements assessment can help guide your preparation decisions and ensure that you are addressing the most important areas for your specific scenario.

Setting Realistic Goals: Pursuing ultimate self-sufficiency in an apocalyptic situation may be impractical and depressing. Instead, create realistic objectives based on your resources and timescale. Begin with necessities such as a 72-hour emergency pack, and steadily increase your readiness over time.

Budget Allocation: Be prepared without breaking the bank. Prioritize necessary goods based on your budget. Use resources like as discounts, bargain retailers, and community preparation initiatives to stretch your budget even further. Remember that even minor efforts in preparation may result in enormous rewards in the event of a catastrophe.

The Prioritization Matrix: Use a prioritization matrix to help you allocate your resources. Consider the significance, cost, and lead time for purchasing certain things. This will allow you to concentrate your efforts on the most significant preparations while remaining within your budget.

Creating Contingency Plans: Responding to Various Disaster Scenarios
Natural catastrophes are unpredictable, requiring flexibility and agility. Creating contingency plans for different situations enables you to react successfully regardless of the nature of the disaster.

Scenario planning: Consider potential catastrophe scenarios that might affect your location. Consider earthquakes, floods, wildfires, and power outages. For each scenario, consider possible problems and specific steps to take.

Family Communication Plan: Create a clear and straightforward strategy for communicating with your family during a crisis. Choose a designated meeting location, arrange backup communication mechanisms such as battery-powered radios or satellite phones, and ensure that everyone knows the plan and their duties within it.

Evacuation Routes: Research and plan probable escape routes from your house and community. Identify alternative routes in case main highways are closed, and make sure everyone in your family is acquainted with the evacuation strategy.

Practice Makes Perfection: Regularly rehearse your backup plans with your family. Use simulated exercises to discover possible gaps or areas for improvement. Familiarity with the strategy will result in a quicker and more efficient reaction during an emergency.

Beyond the Basics: Increasing Community Resilience

Remember that being prepared isn't just about you. Building community resilience via cooperation and information sharing may greatly improve your effectiveness.

Participate in Neighborhood preparation Programs: Many communities have created preparation programs that provide excellent resources and direction. Participate in seminars, training sessions, and community preparation activities to exchange information and resources.

Coordinate with Neighbors: Discuss possible catastrophe scenarios with your neighbors and devise coordinated solutions. Share resources, form mutual help networks, and assign reliable personnel to monitor each other during crises.

Help Local Emergency Services: Volunteer your time and talents to help local disaster response and preparation groups. This might include taking part in search and rescue operations, giving logistical assistance, or aiding with public education projects.

By encouraging collaboration and sharing resources within your community, you can build a network of support and resilience that improves everyone's readiness and reduces the impact of possible catastrophes.

Moving Towards Action:Embracing the Empowered Mindset

Developing a prepared attitude is a continuous effort, not a one-time event. Recognizing and conquering fear, prioritizing your needs and resources, and building flexible contingency plans can change you from a passive spectator to an empowered steward of your own safety and well-being.

Remember that even tiny measures toward preparation may make a big impact in a crisis. Accept the road of developing resilience, establish a proactive mentality, and prepare yourself to meet any situation with confidence and self-reliance. As we go through this book, we'll dig deeper into practical techniques and resources to provide you with the skills and information you need to turn your empowered mentality into real actions that provide a solid basis for successful disaster preparation.

Chapter 3: Stockpiling for Survival—Building Your Emergency Arsenal

When calamity hits, the world you know might come to a standstill. Supermarkets become unavailable, utilities fail under pressure, and basic needs become valuable commodities. In this crucial situation, a well-stocked emergency bag might be the difference between susceptibility and resilience. This chapter looks into the necessary goods to stockpile, providing you with the information and techniques to build a fortress of self-sufficiency in the middle of a storm.

Essential Supplies Checklist: A Lifeline in Uncertainty

Consider the pandemonium of a crisis unfolding: floods blocking off highways, power outages leaving houses in darkness, and communication networks disrupted. In the midst of this uncertainty, your emergency kit serves as a beacon of stability, providing you with the resources you need to sustain yourself and your loved ones until things return to normal. But what should this critical gear include?

The main pillars of survival:
Food: A minimum of 72 hours (preferably 14 days) of non-perishable, calorie-dense food is required. Choose canned foods, protein bars, dried fruits and nuts, and fast meals that need no preparation. When choosing meals, keep in mind your dietary limitations and allergies.
Water: Your body can go weeks without food, but only days without water. Aim for one gallon of water per person each day for drinking, cooking, and cleaning. Invest in water purification pills or filters to assure access to clean water even when sources are contaminated.
Sanitation: Hygiene is critical during crises. Stock up on toilet paper, hand sanitizer, disinfection wipes, and garbage bags. Consider portable sanitation solutions, such as camping toilets or waste disposal bags, if normal facilities are unavailable.
First Aid: Be prepared to treat minor injuries and illnesses. Bandages, antiseptic wipes, pain

relievers, drugs for common ailments (allergies, stomach problems), and any prescription prescriptions your family need should all be included in your pack.

Shelter: Depending on the crisis situation, obtaining temporary shelter may be required. Emergency blankets, tents, tarps, and sleeping bags may all help shield you from the elements.

Beyond the Basics: Tailoring Your Kit to Specific Needs

While the fundamental components mentioned above serve as the basis for any emergency kit, it is critical to customize it to your unique requirements and circumstances. Consider considerations such as:

Family size and composition: Ensure your kit meets the needs of everyone in your household, including children, elderly, and pets.

Dietary restrictions and allergies: Stock up on food and medications for specific dietary needs and allergies within your family.

Medical conditions: If someone in your family has a chronic medical condition, make sure their prescriptions are easily accessible and consider emergency backup plans.

Regional risks: Customize your kit depending on the most common dangers in your region. For example, if floods are an issue, consider waterproof containers and sandbags.

Non-Perishable Food Storage: Keep Your Pantry Prepared

Food is the foundation of survival, and maintaining a sufficient supply of non-perishable foods is critical. Here are some important considerations while creating your emergency food pantry:

Selection: Choose high-calorie, shelf-stable foods such as canned beans, rice, pasta, canned meats and fish, protein bars, dried fruits and nuts, and quick soups. Avoid sugary or highly processed meals that have little nutritional benefit.

Storage: Purchase airtight containers for long-term storage. Glass jars with rubber seals and heavy-duty plastic containers with locking lids are ideal choices. To allow for easier rotation and avoid rotting, label each container with the contents and date purchased.

Rotation: Implement the "first-in, first-out" mechanism. Consume outdated food products from your cupboard on a regular basis while replacing them with fresh ones. This keeps your emergency meals fresh and easily accessible.

Cooking Options: Don't forget your cooking gear! Include a portable camp stove, fuel canisters, a mess kit, and utensils in your bag so you may cook meals even when standard cooking facilities are unavailable.

Water Purification and Conservation Techniques: Bringing Every Drop to Life

Safe drinking water is a must during any calamity. While bottled water might be useful at first, it is not a long-term solution. Therefore, knowing water purification and conservation procedures becomes critical:

Water Purification: Purchase water purification pills, filters, or portable UV filtering equipment. These equipment can safely treat tainted water, providing access to clean drinking water even when normal sources are disrupted.

Water Storage: Keep water in clean, BPA-free containers such as Nalgene bottles, jugs, or water barrels. To prioritize the consumption of older water, label each container with the date it was filled.

Conservation Methods: During an emergency, use water conservation methods. Take shorter showers, reuse cooking water, and reduce water waste.

Every drop saved may help to increase your water reserves and guarantee long-term sustainability. Consider rainwater gathering methods if possible in your area. Remember, education is your most powerful weapon against water shortage. Familiarize yourself with your local water sources and any contaminants.

Going Beyond the Basics: Advanced Water Procurement and Treatment

For protracted crisis scenarios or circumstances when easily accessible water supplies are significantly degraded, sophisticated water procurement and treatment solutions may be required:

Water collection bags: Purchase heavy-duty water collection bags that may be used to collect rainfall or runoff from rooftops and other surfaces.

Water purification pills: These widely available tablets successfully remove hazardous bacteria and protozoa in polluted water, making it safe to drink. Remember that they may not eliminate viruses or chemicals.

Portable water filters: For more complete filtration, choose filters made of ceramic, charcoal, or reverse osmosis membrane. Investigate alternatives for various sorts of pollutants and their efficacy in combating possible problems in your area.

Water distillation: Boiling water for at least one minute is efficient in killing most germs and viruses. However, distillation is an energy-intensive process that may not be accessible in certain emergency circumstances.

Alternative Power Sources and Off-Grid Solutions: Light the Way Through Darkness
Power outages are a regular occurrence in the aftermath of many natural catastrophes, leaving

houses in darkness and hampering crucial functions. To retain your autonomy and well-being, consider including alternate power sources into your preparation plan:

Solar Power: Portable solar panels and rechargeable batteries may offer clean and renewable energy for charging electronics, powering small appliances, and even turning on LED lights. Invest on solar chargers for smartphones, tablets, and other vital electrical devices.

Generators: While generators provide more electricity than solar panels, they need fuel and may not be appropriate for all circumstances. When using generators, ensure that there is enough ventilation and that noise levels do not annoy neighbors or draw unwanted attention.

Battery storage: Invest in rechargeable batteries of varying sizes to meet diverse power requirements. Battery-powered lanterns, radios, and flashlights may offer critical illumination and communication during power outages.

Alternative Cooking techniques: If typical cooking techniques are unavailable, camping stoves, propane grills, or even portable fire pits may offer an alternative. When utilizing open flames inside or in restricted places, always put safety and sufficient ventilation first.

Beyond the Basics: Advanced Off-grid Solutions Individuals living in rural places or pursuing a complete off-grid lifestyle may benefit from investigating more sophisticated alternatives.

Wind turbines: Portable wind turbines may use wind power to create energy, but their practicality is dependent on wind patterns in your area.
Biogas digesters: These systems convert organic waste into biogas, which is a sustainable energy source that may be used to cook, heat, or generate power. However, they need room and specialized management skills.
Micro-hydropower systems: For people with access to flowing water sources, micro-hydropower systems may be a feasible alternative for producing energy on a small scale. The practicality and possible environmental effect of such systems should be thoroughly assessed.

Communication in Chaos: Staying Connected Even When the Grid Is Down

Maintaining communication during and after a crisis is critical for coordinating with loved ones, obtaining emergency assistance, and keeping up with events. Instead than depending on possibly unstable cell networks, explore alternate communication methods:

Battery-powered Radios: AM/FM radios operated by batteries or hand cranks may still give access to news and emergency broadcasts when infrastructure is down. Models with NOAA weather alert capability provide real-time updates during severe weather occurrences.

Satellite phones: While they need a subscription and may have limited coverage, satellite phones provide dependable communication even when traditional networks are offline. They may be quite useful for contacting emergency services or communicating with distant family members.

Offline Communication Tools: Consider pre-downloading maps, emergency contact lists, and other information to your mobile devices so you can access them even when you don't have an internet connection. Use pre-arranged communication procedures with family members, such as defined meeting locations or radio frequency for check-ins.

Community Communication Boards: If possible, set up community communication boards or dedicated messaging centers in your area. These may act as primary centers for information exchange and updates during an emergency.

Chapter 4: Fortifying Your Home and Property: Building a Bastion Against the Storm

When natural calamities strike, your house should provide more than simply shelter; it should be a stronghold of resistance. This chapter digs into the art of reinforcing your property, changing it from a possible risk to a source of protection and security against a variety of dangers.

Structural Reinforcements: Standing Firm in the Face of Fury

Different calamities provide distinct difficulties to your home's structural integrity. Let's look at particular reinforcement techniques for frequent threats:

Earthquake bracing:

Foundation Bolting: To minimize shifting and movement during earthquakes, secure your house's foundation to the underlying bedrock. Consult structural professionals for the best anchoring solutions depending on your home's structure and regional seismic threats.

Wall Strapping: To avoid wall collapse due to shear stresses, install bracing straps diagonally across internal walls and external framework. Use high-quality metal straps and anchor them according to the approved ways.

Furniture Securing: Anchor furniture such as bookcases, cabinets, and appliances to avoid toppling and injury during earthquakes. Use furniture straps, L-brackets, or earthquake putty to fasten objects to walls or floors.

Flood Mitigation:

Sealing Entry Points: Seal cracks and openings around doors, windows, and utility lines to keep water out. Use waterproof sealants, weatherstripping, and door sweeps to form a watertight barrier.

Elevation Strategies: Consider elevating your house, particularly if you reside in a flood-prone location. The options include elevating the base, building on stilts, or erecting flood-resistant barriers around the perimeter.

Backflow Prevention: Add backflow prevention valves to your plumbing system to keep flood water from backing up into your drains and polluting your water supply.

Windproofing Strategy:
Roof Reinforcement: Inspect and strengthen your roof to improve wind resistance. Secure any loose shingles, flashing, or vents, and consider using impact-resistant roofing materials in high-risk locations.
Window and Door Protection: Use storm shutters or impact-resistant windows and doors to protect against strong winds and flying debris. Use hurricane straps and bracing hardware to brace doors and keep them from blowing open.
Debris Mitigation: Trim overhanging branches and remove loose things from your property, such as yard furniture or grills, to prevent them from becoming missiles in severe winds.

When carrying out large structural reinforcements, contact with certified specialists such as structural engineers or contractors. Their knowledge will guarantee that your renovations are suited to your individual home and adhere to local building requirements.

Essential Home Modifications: Adapting to the Unexpected
Aside from basic fortifications, various changes might improve your home's utility and flexibility during crises.

Fire Escape Ladders: Install fire escape ladders in your house to give alternate evacuation routes in the event of a fire or a blocked stairs. Choose ladders that are appropriate for your building's height and readily accessible from higher stories. Emergency Shelters: Consider creating designated safe rooms or reinforced places in your house to guard against particular hazards such as tornadoes or severe weather occurrences. Shelters should be structurally sound, well-ventilated, and stocked with essential supplies. Consider investing in backup generators for power outages, sump pumps for flooding, and alternative heating sources such as wood-burning stoves or fireplaces for situations where regular utilities are unavailable.*Water Storage and Treatment:**

Install water storage tanks and investigate water purifying equipment to assure availability to safe drinking water even if municipal supplies are disrupted. Regularly inspect and test your water treatment equipment.

Securing Valuables and Documents: Protecting Your Treasure
Natural catastrophes not only damage physical buildings, but also valuable possessions and priceless records. Implementing comprehensive security measures is critical.

Fireproof Safes: Purchase fireproof safes with proper temperature and water resistance ratings to secure important papers, valuables, and treasured mementos. Securely fasten the safes to the ground or walls to avoid theft during evacuations.
Waterproof Caches: Use waterproof containers or pouches to protect essential papers, photos, and electronic material from flood damage. Store these caches in elevated or flood-proof areas of your home.
Digital backups: Make digital backups of crucial papers, financial information, and irreplaceable

personal files to external hard drives or cloud storage systems. To reduce the chance of loss, keep your backups updated on a regular basis and store them elsewhere.

Beyond the Basics: Advanced Fortification Strategies
Individuals living in high-risk locations or wanting complete preparation may benefit from investigating sophisticated fortification measures.

Retrofitting for Earthquake Resilience: Speak with structural experts about retrofitting procedures such as seismic straps, base isolation systems, and foundation strengthening measures to greatly improve your home's earthquake resistance.
Floodproofing Techniques: Depending on your budget and risk tolerance, you should consider modern flood-proofing techniques such as flood doors, automated sealing systems, and waterproof membranes for walls and foundations. These unique systems provide exceptional flood protection.

Hurricane Resistant Construction: If you live in a hurricane-prone location, employing hurricane-resistant materials and construction practices may greatly increase your home's capacity to withstand strong winds and flying debris. Consult architects and builders that specialize in hurricane-resistant buildings for advice.

Self-sustaining Features: For those looking for long-term resilience and off-grid capabilities, consider designing your house with rainwater collection, solar power generating, and greywater recycling systems. These qualities may considerably lessen your dependency on external infrastructure while increasing your self-sufficiency during long-term situations.

Maintaining and Monitoring Your Fortifications: Vigilance Is Essential

Fortifying your house is a continuous effort, not a one-time event. To keep your defenses effective, use these practices:

Regular Inspections: Check your fortifications on a regular basis for indications of wear or damage. Check the roof's integrity, foundation stability, and backup system functionality. To provide maximum protection, address any faults as soon as possible.

Documents and Maintenance Logs: Keep thorough records of all fortification measures, including installation dates, materials utilized, and equipment maintenance schedules. This information will be useful for future reference and may aid insurance companies with damage claims.

Community Collaboration: Collaborate with your neighbors to reinforce shared spaces and develop joint response strategies. Sharing resources and skills may help your community become more resilient.

Chapter 5: Building Community Resilience - We are stronger together than alone.

Individual planning is important, but the ultimate strength of resilience rests in community effort. This chapter looks into the notion of community resilience, demonstrating how working with your neighbors may greatly improve your preparation and response skills in the event of a catastrophe.

Neighborhood Preparedness Initiatives: Creating a Web of Support
Imagine that in the middle of a tragedy, your neighbors had your back. They exchange resources, provide aid, and collaborate to overcome obstacles. This is the core of community preparedness: a proactive strategy in which members of a community work together to plan, prepare, and react efficiently to catastrophes.

Collaborative Planning:

Organize Neighborhood Preparedness Meetings: Gather your neighbors and start talking about shared dangers, strengths, and weaknesses. Consider alternative circumstances and collaborate to establish reaction strategies.

Create Neighborhood reaction Teams: Identify people with unique talents and resources, such as medical professionals, handymen, and communication specialists, and assign positions within designated reaction teams. This facilitates timely reaction and resource allocation during an emergency.

Establish Communication Networks: Set up communication channels such as community radio frequencies, internet forums, or even specialized bulletin boards to exchange information, organize help, and stay in touch during crises.

Resource sharing:

Create a Community Resource Inventory: Compile a comprehensive inventory of community members' talents, resources, and emergency supplies. This inventory may be very useful in identifying available resources and organizing requirements during catastrophes.

Organize Community Stockpiles: Establish common emergency supply caches including critical supplies like water, food, first-aid kits, and tools. This community stockpile may augment individual preparation while ensuring crucial supplies are readily accessible.

Skill-Sharing Workshops: Plan workshops where people may exchange their knowledge on topics such as first aid, fire safety, and simple repairs. This information sharing strengthens the community and promotes self-sufficiency amid catastrophes.

Communications networks:

Establish Neighborhood Watch Programs: Create a collaborative watch program in which neighbors keep an eye out for suspicious activities or possible risks, therefore improving overall community safety and preparedness.

Utilize Technology Platforms: Set up online platforms or mobile applications to facilitate community communication, resource sharing, and real-time information during crises.

Remember to have offline communication backups in case technology fails.

frequent Drills and Simulations: Hold frequent drills and simulations to test your community response plans, identify areas for improvement, and acquaint everyone with their roles and responsibilities.

Familiarity with Local Emergency Plans and Evacuation Routes: Understanding the way out and in

Beyond your own community efforts, knowing and incorporating into current municipal emergency preparations is critical. Here's what you should know.

Local emergency plans: Familiarize yourself with your local emergency plan. Determine the approved evacuation routes, emergency shelters, and communication methods set by authorities. Knowing the official response framework allows your community initiatives to effectively connect with larger disaster response organizations.

Evacuation routes: Map out major and secondary evacuation routes from your community, taking into account probable interruptions like floods or debris. Share these routes with your neighbors and practice them often. Determine alternate modes of transportation in case personal automobiles are unavailable.

Emergency Contact Details: Keep an easily available list of emergency contact information, such as local authorities, emergency agencies, designated family members, and community leaders. Share this information with your neighbors so that everyone has access to it, even if there is a power outage or a communication disturbance.

Engaging Family and Friends: Educating, Training, and Developing a Prepared Team
Preparedness begins at home. Engaging your family and friends in preparation initiatives promotes an awareness culture and provides a united reaction unit in the event of an emergency.

Education and Awareness: Inform your family and friends about possible threats in your community, emergency response strategies, and personal preparation actions. Share information and resources so that everyone is on the same page.

Training and Drills: Hold practice drills at home to simulate various catastrophe situations and practice evacuation procedures, communication protocols, and first-aid practices. This familiarity and coordination may be quite beneficial in an emergency.

Creating a Family Emergency Kit: Work with your family to create a comprehensive emergency kit that meets everyone's individual needs and dietary requirements. Ensure that the kit is easily accessible and that everyone knows where it is located.

Delegation of Responsibilities: During an emergency, assign clear duties and responsibilities among members of your household. This might include communicating with neighbors, organizing supplies, delivering first aid, or looking after vulnerable members. Having a clear strategy allows everyone to participate successfully during difficult moments.

Remember, strengthening community resilience is a continuous effort, not a one-time event. Regularly evaluate your plans, update information, and participate in community preparation initiatives. The more robust your community's support and cooperation network is, the better it will be able to weather any storm.

Beyond the Basics: Growing Your Community's Resilience Efforts
For towns looking to further increase their readiness and response skills, researching these advanced efforts may be beneficial:

Vulnerability Assessments: Perform detailed vulnerability assessments to identify particular gaps and opportunities for improvement in your community's preparation infrastructure. This research may help guide focused resource allocation and choose activities with the greatest benefit.
Resilience Grant Programs: Look into grant programs and financing options that assist community preparation projects. Use these resources to purchase equipment, create

training programs, or undertake infrastructure modifications that will strengthen your community's resilience.

Collaborations with Local Organizations: Form collaborations with local institutions such as schools, medical facilities, and non-profit organizations. These alliances may broaden resource pools, provide specialized skills, and establish a larger network of assistance during an emergency.

mentoring and Knowledge Sharing: Establish mentoring programs in your community so that experienced preparation professionals may share their knowledge and abilities with newbies. This encourages a culture of continuity and guarantees that preparation information is handed along to future generations.

Advocacy and Policy Engagement: At the local and regional levels, advocate for policies and laws that improve disaster readiness and resilience. Lobby for financing, infrastructure upgrades, and educational activities that benefit your town while also improving overall readiness.

Remember, developing community resilience is about more than just preparing for imminent calamities; it's about instilling a culture of readiness and self-reliance in daily life. By incorporating preparation ideas into community events, educational programs, and even recreational activities, you can establish a long-term foundation for resilience, empowering your community to handle not just catastrophes but also the difficulties of a changing world.

Case Studies on Community Resilience:
Community-driven initiatives helped revitalize areas and develop long-term resilience during New Orleans' post-Katrina reconstruction efforts. The Sendai Framework for Disaster Risk Reduction promotes community-centered disaster preparation and resilience development.
Indigenous communities throughout the globe have launched resilience efforts that rely on traditional knowledge and traditions to adapt to environmental changes and natural dangers.

Part 2: Weathering the Storm

Chapter 6: Emergency Alert and Early Warning Systems - Managing Uncertainty via Knowledge and Action

When weather systems turn into roaring storms and natural disasters threaten, quick knowledge and prompt action become critical components of survival. This chapter digs into the critical domain of emergency alert and early warning systems, providing you with the information and methods needed to handle the sometimes chaotic world of incoming dangers.

Monitor Weather and Hazard Predictions: From Data to Actionable Plans

In the age of knowledge, a profusion of meteorological data and danger projections overwhelm us from many sources. Navigating this terrain successfully requires:

Reliable sources:

National meteorological Service (NWS): The NWS, a government body, provides official forecasts, watches, and warnings for a variety of meteorological events. Use their website, mobile app, and radio broadcasts to get authoritative and real-time information.

Local News and Government Agency: Local news networks and government websites often give hyper-localized information and updates particular to your location. Trust credible sources with a track record of truthful reporting.

Scientific and Academic Resources: Research institutes and respectable scientific organizations may provide detailed analysis and specialized predictions for certain kinds of dangers. Use these resources to get a better knowledge and perspective.

Interpretation and Action Plan:

Understanding Terminology: Learn crucial phrases such as watches, warnings, and advisories so that you can appropriately evaluate the severity and urgency of forecasts.

The NWS website offers extensive glossaries and explanations.

Mapping Tools: Use online mapping and weather visualization platforms to follow storm trajectories, see anticipated effects, and locate probable evacuation zones.

Personalize Your Response: Convert predictions and warnings into tailored action plans for your scenario. When developing your reaction plan, consider issues such as your location, susceptibility, and resource availability.

Remember that knowledge is not power until it is put into action. Monitor credible sources on a regular basis, properly evaluate information, and create individual reaction strategies depending on changing circumstances.

Understanding Official Alerts and Evacuation Orders: Responding Quickly and Coordinated

Official warnings and evacuation orders are key turning moments in the face of imminent danger. Responding quickly and effectively is critical:

Types of Alerts:

Watches: Indicate that a dangerous occurrence may occur within a certain period. Stay informed, keep track of events, and plan for possible action.

Warnings: Indicate the upcoming occurrence of a dangerous event in your region. Start your pre-determined action plan right away, which may include finding shelter, safeguarding your property, or leaving.

Evacuation Orders: Order the prompt evacuation of a specified location due to impending danger. Do not delay; evacuate immediately via authorized routes to prepared shelters.

Coordination and communication:

Emergency Broadcasts: Listen closely to radio and television broadcasts for official notifications and updates. Follow instructions from emergency personnel and authorized officials.

Community Communication Networks: Use existing community communication channels, such as neighborhood forums or websites, to keep informed and coordinate activities with your neighbors.

Family Communication Plan: Ensure that everyone in your family is aware of the specified communication channels and meeting spots in the event of an evacuation or a breakdown in normal communications.

Ttimely and coordinated action may considerably increase your odds of survival and reduce possible damage. To successfully handle the crisis, evacuate when directed, keep updated via reputable means, and collaborate with your community.

Alternative Communication Strategies: Staying Connected When the Grid is Down

Natural catastrophes often damage traditional communication networks, isolating populations and preventing critical information flow. Alternative communication tactics become necessary in such situations:

Emergency Radios: Purchase a battery-powered or hand-crank emergency radio with NOAA weather alert features. These radios enable access to crucial updates and emergency bulletins even when power is down.

Satellite phones: While satellite phones provide greater connection dependability, they cost subscriptions and may have restricted coverage in certain places. Consider their efficacy and cost-benefit in your individual circumstance.

Offline Messages: Pre-download offline maps, contact information, and emergency procedures to your mobile devices. Use pre-made message templates and scheduled meeting places with family and neighbors to promote communication even when there is no internet connection.

Community Communication Boards: If possible, set up dedicated community communication boards or bulletin boards in central areas. These may act as information centers for updates, messaging, and coordination during an emergency.

Redundancy and flexibility are essential.

Use a variety of communication methods to improve your chances of remaining connected amid interruptions. Test your devices on a regular basis, have backup power sources handy, and practice using alternate communication channels.

Beyond the Basics: Advanced Alert and Response System
Individuals living in high-risk locations or wanting thorough preparation may benefit from studying enhanced alert and response systems.

Community-Based Early Warning Systems: Local communities may set up their own early warning systems, using sensor networks, citizen science data, and traditional knowledge to supplement official forecasts and give hyper-localized hazard predictions. Consider engaging in or supporting similar activities in your community.

Real-Time Monitoring Technology: Cutting-edge technology such as remote sensing and satellite images provide real-time information on phenomena such as floodwater levels, wildfire propagation, and volcanic activity. Accessing services that use this data may give extra insights and situational awareness.

Personal Alert Systems: Invest in personal alert systems such as weather radios with location-specific warnings or wearable sensors that send out notifications for approaching risks such as earthquakes or landslides. These may provide individualized protection and rapid knowledge, particularly in cases when official warnings may be delayed.

*Smart Home Technology: Connect smart home systems to emergency alerts. Automated systems that respond to signals by turning off utilities, locking doors, or adjusting environmental controls may help to reduce damage and increase safety during catastrophes.

Sophisticated systems are only tools. Their performance is dependent on a thorough knowledge, integration into your entire preparation strategy, and frequent maintenance. Check compatibility with your local infrastructure and emergency response methods.

Case Studies for Effective Alert and Response Systems:

The Indian Ocean Tsunami Early Warning System is a network of buoys and tidal gauges that delivers critical tsunami alerts across the Indian Ocean area.

The Sendai Framework for Disaster Risk Reduction prioritizes community-based early warning systems and public involvement in disaster preparation.

The effectiveness of storm preparation and evacuation activities in coastal cities that have invested in strong public education, communication infrastructure, and well-organized response plans.

These examples demonstrate how good alarm and response systems may save lives and minimize damage. You may help to create a safer and more resilient environment for yourself and people around you by remaining educated on improvements, advocating for strong systems in your community, and appropriately using available technologies.

Chapter 7: Taking Action During Different Disasters—Navigating the Chaos with Knowledge and Calm

When nature unleashes its wrath in the form of earthquakes, floods, hurricanes, or wildfires, preparedness and quick thinking become your most valuable assets. This chapter looks into particular safety procedures and reaction techniques adapted to distinct catastrophe situations, helping you to make educated choices and protect yourself and your loved ones during times of crisis.

Earthquake Safety Procedures: When the Ground Rumbles Under Your Feet
Even the most courageous people might be terrified by an earthquake's shocks. However, a strong awareness of safety measures may make a huge difference:

Drop, Cover, and Hold: the golden rule. When the earth shakes, drop to the ground and seek cover behind a substantial piece of furniture, such as a desk or table, holding on until the shaking stops. Avoid glass, mirrors, and hanging things that may shatter and cause damage.

Fire Extinguishment: Earthquakes may damage gas pipes and start fires. If a fire breaks out, examine the situation immediately. If the fire is small and confined, try extinguishing it using a fire extinguisher designed for that sort of fire. Prioritize your safety and exit immediately if the fire is huge and spreading quickly.

Evacuation Procedures: Prepare for any aftershocks after the shaking has stopped. Familiarize yourself with your building's evacuation strategy and exits. Evacuate calmly and methodically, avoiding elevators owing to possible power shortages. Once outdoors, stay away from buildings and overhead dangers like power wires or trees.

Earthquakes may impair communication networks. Have a pre-arranged meeting place with your family outside your house in case you get separated. Stay informed with battery-powered radios or communal communication channels.

Flood Response Strategy: When Water Rises with Wrath
Floods may devastate homes and communities. Knowing how to respond can reduce damage and keep you safe:

Moving to higher ground: The most important thing to do during a flood is to instantly seek higher ground. If you live in a flood-prone region, prepare ahead of time to find higher ground and develop an evacuation plan. Do not drive over flooded roadways since the river might quickly sweep cars away.

Securing Your Belongings: Before floods approach your house, relocate valuable possessions and furniture to higher floors. Elevate appliances and gadgets to reduce water damage. Seal and sandbag doors and windows to keep water out. To prevent possible risks, turn off all utilities, such as power and gas.

Turning off utilities: As floods approach, turn off your main water valve and gas supply line to avoid leaks and even explosions. You may need to contact your utility provider for help. Avoid touching electrical equipment while standing in water or with wet hands.

Floodwaters may be polluted with sewage and trash. If you have no choice but to wade through floods, use appropriate clothes and boots. Be aware of concealed risks such as submerged electrical wires or fragile buildings.

Hurricane Preparedness and Survival: When Winds Release Their Fury
Hurricanes bring severe winds, storm surges, and heavy rains, necessitating extensive planning and early action.

Boarding Up Windows: Use plywood or hurricane shutters to protect your windows from shattered debris. This reduces wind damage and keeps flying items from entering your property.

Storm Surge Awareness: Understand the possibility for storm surge in your region. Identify evacuation zones and make plans to evacuate to higher ground if required. Storm surges have the potential to flood coastal communities even if the hurricane makes landfall elsewhere.

Sheltering options: If evacuation is not an option, locate a secure space in your house, ideally an inside room on the lowest floor with no windows. Stock this area with emergency supplies and make sure everyone in your household is aware of its location.

Follow official channels for updates on the hurricane's trajectory and strength. Avoid going outdoors during the storm unless absolutely essential. After the storm, be aware of fallen power lines, damaged buildings, and probable floods.

Wildfire Evacuation and Protection Measures: When Fires Paint the Sky Red

Wildfires can spread quickly, destroying landscapes and endangering populations. Recognizing the indications and responding quickly are critical:

Creating Firebreaks: If you have the time, try building fire breaks around your home by cleaning combustible plants and trash. This may assist to halt the fire's spread and safeguard your property.

Planning Escape Routes: Identify numerous escape routes from your property, including main and secondary choices in the event of a closed path. Clear these paths of any impediments and make sure everyone in your household is acquainted with them.

Securing the Property: Close all windows and doors to prevent embers from entering your house. Turn off the propane tanks and gas pipes. If a fire is threatening your home, remove combustible things and try wetting down your roof and external walls.

Evacuation is often the safest choice during wildfires. If authorities advise you to leave or if the fire offers an imminent danger to your safety, do so without hesitation. Stay up to speed on fires and evacuation orders by following trusted sources.

Further Considerations for Specific Disasters:
Tornadoes: Take quick cover in a basement or inside room on the lowest level, away from windows and doors. Lie down on the ground and cover your head and neck with your arms. If found outside, lay down in a ditch or depression away from trees and electricity wires.
Landslides: Look for symptoms of a landslide, such as fissures in the ground, bending trees, or moist dirt. If you fear a landslide is about to occur, evacuate the area immediately.
Chemical spills: Follow emergency personnel's directions for evacuation or sheltering in situ. Wear protective clothes and avoid making contact with the spilled liquid.

Going Beyond the Basics: Advanced Disaster Response Strategies

Individuals wanting thorough preparation and living in high-risk locations may benefit from investigating advanced disaster response tactics.

First-Aid and CPR Training: Learn basic first-aid and CPR techniques to deal with injuries and crises during catastrophes, particularly if medical help is delayed.

Search and Rescue procedures: Consider getting training in basic search and rescue procedures to help yourself and others in the event of a building collapse or trapped persons.

Ham Radio Operator Training: Learning to use a ham radio may give communication capabilities even when traditional networks are unavailable, allowing you to communicate with emergency services or other communities.

Disaster Preparedness for Pets and Livestock: Create detailed plans for your pets' and livestock's safety and well-being during catastrophes, such as evacuation routes, sheltering choices, and emergency supplies.

Knowledge is power, and skills are vital assets in an emergency. Invest in training, acquire appropriate equipment, and practice response strategies on a regular basis to improve your preparedness and response capabilities.

Case Studies for Effective Disaster Response:
The 2015 Nepal earthquake response relied heavily on community-based early warning systems and trained volunteers. The successful evacuation of coastal areas during Hurricane Florence in 2018 emphasizes the need of public education, strong communication networks, and adequate evacuation strategies. Following the 2011 Tohoku earthquake and tsunami in Japan, community-driven post-disaster recovery activities demonstrated communities' resilience and collaborative spirit in reconstructing their lives.

These examples highlight the value of early planning, informed action, and collaborative efforts in limiting catastrophe consequences and building community resilience. By learning from these triumphs and customizing your reaction techniques to your individual situation, you can help to create a safer and better prepared community for yourself and future generations

Chapter 8: First Aid and Medical Preparedness—Mending Body and Mind in the Face of Crisis

When calamity hits, medical infrastructure and access to healthcare might be jeopardized. This chapter provides you with the information and resources you need to handle such circumstances, allowing you to offer critical first aid, manage medical demands, and protect the mental and emotional well-being of yourself and others in the aftermath of an emergency.

Essential First-Aid Kit Contents: A Portable Lifeline
A well-stocked first-aid kit serves as your first line of defense in an emergency. Create a thorough pack adapted to your unique requirements and surroundings, ensuring that it includes the following items.

Medications:
Use over-the-counter pain medicines such acetaminophen, ibuprofen, or naproxen to

manage discomfort and fever. Antihistamines may help with allergy symptoms and bug bites.
Gastrointestinal drugs: Anti-diarrhea and antacids for digestive issues.
Prescription medications: Maintain an adequate supply of any necessary prescription medications for self and family members.

Wound-Care Supplies:
- Antiseptic wipes and solutions to clean wounds and prevent infection.
- Bandages and gauze pads in different sizes to dress wounds of varying severity.
- Adhesive tape and roller bandages to secure dressings and provide support.
- Wound closure strips for minor cuts that require approximation.
- Tweezers and sterile scissors to remove splinters and debris.

Trauma-Management Tools:
- Instant cold packs for pain relief and swelling reduction from sprains and strains.
- Triangular bandages and slings for immobilizing arms and shoulders.

- Splints and braces for immobilizing fractures and sprains.
- Emergency blanket to maintain body heat in case of hypothermia.
- Personal protective equipment (PPE) such as gloves, masks, and eye protection for handling bodily fluids safely.

Additional Consideration:

Personalize your kit: Include medications or supplies for specific needs, such as allergies, chronic conditions, or children's needs.

Organize for easy access: Label and compartmentalize your kit for efficient supply retrieval during emergencies. Refresh and restock regularly: Check expiry dates and replace any used goods in your kit. Include a checklist for easier inventory management.

Training is important: Familiarity with basic first-aid methods increases the usefulness of your gear. Invest in first-aid training to improve your abilities.

A well-stocked first-aid kit is an investment in your personal readiness as well as the safety of others during an emergency.

Prioritize its assembly and make sure everyone in your household is aware of its location and how to use its contents.

Basic Life Support Skills: When Every Minute Matters

Beyond supplies, equipping oneself with crucial life support skills may make a significant impact in saving lives:

Cardiopulmonary resuscitation (CPR):

Master the fundamentals of chest compressions, rescue breaths, and airway management. Regularly practice CPR on manikins or take refresher classes. Individuals suffering cardiac arrest who get early and efficient CPR have a much higher probability of survival.

Wound Care and Bleeding Control:

Understand various kinds of wounds and suitable dressing treatments. Apply direct pressure to stop bleeding until medical help arrives.

Tourniquets should only be used as a last resort when extremity bleeding is serious and life-threatening. Learn the right application approaches and restrictions.

Emergency Response Techniques:
Recognize the symptoms of shock, hypothermia, and hyperthermia. Understand basic intervention strategies for stabilizing the person until medical aid comes.
Learn how to transfer and position wounded people properly, preventing additional injury.

Basic life support skills can make the difference between life and death in critical situations. Invest in training, practice often, and maintain confidence in your ability to respond decisively in an emergency.

Managing Mental and Emotional Health: Beyond Physical Wounds
Disasters affect not only our physical health, but also our mental and emotional well-being. Recognizing and resolving these issues is critical for long-term healing.

Manage Stress and Anxiety:

Recognize common stress symptoms, such as difficulty sleeping, changes in appetite, irritability, and difficulty concentrating.

Practice relaxation techniques, such as deep breathing exercises, meditation, yoga, or spending time in nature, to manage stress and anxiety.

Connect and share.

Seek help from trustworthy friends, family members, or mental health experts by sharing your experiences and feelings.

Dealing with Trauma:

Acknowledge and validate your feelings: Allow yourself to experience the full spectrum of emotions that might develop after a traumatic event. Bottling things up might impede healing.

Seek professional assistance: If you are experiencing chronic emotions of dread, melancholy, or hopelessness, get professional mental health help. Therapists may provide skills and methods for dealing with trauma and the emotional repercussions of catastrophes.

Develop resilience: Engage in activities that promote general well-being, such as regular exercise, nutritious food, and a consistent sleep routine. These techniques help to build emotional resilience and improve your capacity to deal with stress and obstacles.

Supporting Others:
Be a good listener: Create a secure environment for people to express their experiences and feelings without being judged. To support individuals, practice active listening and validate their feelings. Offer practical assistance, such as childcare, cooking, or errands, to alleviate their burden. Also, connect them with resources, such as mental health services, support groups, or community resources.

Mental and emotional well-being are equally as important as physical health in the aftermath of disasters.
Prioritize self-care, seek help when necessary, and be kind and understanding to yourself and others as you handle any emotional problems that may occur.

Increasing Community Resilience:
Addressing mental and emotional well-being demands a collaborative effort. Community members may contribute by:

Promoting mental health awareness and education: Host seminars, presentations, and resource fairs to inform community people about common mental health issues and accessible help.
Creating support networks: Form peer support groups or online forums where people may interact, share their experiences, and give mutual encouragement.
Advocating for mental health resources: Advocate for more funding and access to mental health services in your community, guaranteeing enough support for everybody.

By creating a caring and understanding atmosphere, communities can help people recover, restore their emotional well-being, and contribute to a more resilient future for everyone.

Part III: Reconstruction and Recovery

Chapter 9: Assessing Damage and Initial Response—Navigating the Aftermath with Courage and Clarity

When the dust settles after a calamity, the difficult process of rebuilding starts. To navigate the early reaction phase, you must prioritize your safety, communicate efficiently with authorities, and properly record losses in order to facilitate quick recovery.

Personal Safety First: Prioritizing Your Well-Being During Chaos

Before even analyzing the magnitude of the damage, your first attention should be on safeguarding your own and others' safety:

Checking for hazards:

Structural Integrity: Determine the stability of your surroundings. Look for cracked walls, collapsing roofs, and damaged windows. If your house looks to be structurally vulnerable, do not enter and seek other refuge.

Downed Power Lines and Live Wires: Keep away from any downed power lines or sparking electrical equipment. Report them right away to the utility provider or emergency services.

Gas Leaks: Be aware of the smell of gas, which signals a possible leak. Turn off the main gas valve if possible and promptly exit the area, warning others and emergency personnel.

Fire dangers: Be aware of possible fire dangers such as sparking wires, smoldering trash, and flammable items. If it is safe, extinguish minor flames; nevertheless, if the fire is big or spreading, prioritize evacuation.

Biological Hazards: Floods and sewage leaks may pollute water and surfaces with pathogenic microorganisms. When wading through floods, use protective gear and footwear to prevent coming into touch with potentially hazardous things.

Your safety comes first. Proceed with care, prioritize evacuation if required, and do not hesitate to call emergency services for help in identifying any threats.

Calling Emergency Services and Authorities: Requesting Assistance and Reporting Damage
Once the immediate threat has passed, it is critical to notify authorities about the event and seek any required assistance:

Emergency Services: Contact emergency services for life-threatening situations, injuries, or potential hazards.
Local Authorities: Report property damage to your local emergency management agency or disaster relief authorities.
Utilities: Notify utility companies of any disruptions, such as power outages, gas leaks, or broken water lines, to expedite repairs and restore services.
Insurance Companies: Contact your insurance company to begin the claims process and document the damage for future reference.

Clear and timely communication is critical. Provide precise information about your location, the nature of the damage, and any urgent requirements so that resources and help may be sent efficiently.

Documenting Losses and Damages: Establishing a Comprehensive Record for Recovery
Thorough documenting of losses and damages is critical in easing insurance claims, financial aid programs, and rebuilding efforts.

Photographs and Video Footage: Gather thorough visual proof of the damage to your property, both inside and out. Take close-up photographs of selected locations and use appropriate lighting for clarity.
Written Records: Make a detailed list of all damaged or destroyed personal belongings, including condition, approximate value, and brand names. Receipts and Documentation: Collect any relevant receipts, purchase records, or repair estimates to support your claims.
Official Reports: Obtain copies of official reports submitted by emergency services or

authorities that detail the catastrophe and the degree of damage in your region.

Detailed documentation enhances your claims and makes recovery procedures go more smoothly. Keep copies of all records in a secure place, both physically and digitally, to guarantee their availability in the event of an unanticipated occurrence.

Beyond the Basics: Leveraging Technology for Effective Assessment and Documentation
Advances in technology provide new instruments for detailed examination and documentation:

Drone Photography: If authorized, consider employing drones to film aerial video of the damage to your property, which will provide a larger view and allow for careful investigation of inaccessible regions.
Mobile applications: Several disaster preparation applications enable you to record damage, report to authorities, and connect with support services, therefore expediting the initial reaction process.

internet Documentation Platforms: Use secure internet platforms to save and share images, videos, and written records of your losses, making them easily accessible to insurance companies, disaster relief organizations, and yourself.

Technology may be a helpful asset in navigating the early reaction phase. Look into available tools and use them appropriately to improve the speed and accuracy of your assessment and documentation efforts.

Case Studies for Effective Initial Response:
The coordinated response to Nepal's 2015 earthquake, in which communities used local knowledge and technology such as drones to survey damage and enable focused rescue operations.
Implemented efficient documentation and claims process following Hurricane Harvey in 2017, using online platforms and simplified processes to reduce processing delays and allocate resources more effectively. The collaborative strategy used during the

Australian bushfires in 2020, where government, communities, and technology
The collaborative strategy used during the 2020 Australian bushfires, in which government, communities, and technology businesses collaborated to create real-time fire maps and evacuation plans, resulting in fewer fatalities and more effective fire control.

These examples demonstrate the value of clear communication, excellent documentation, and leveraging available resources during the early reaction phase. By learning from previous recovery efforts and tailoring techniques to your individual situation, you may manage the immediate aftermath of a tragedy with more efficiency and resilience.

Moving Forward: From Assessment To Recovery
The first reaction phase serves as the basis for the long-term healing process. By putting safety first, communicating effectively, and thoroughly recording losses, you empower yourself to navigate the path ahead with clarity and purpose. Remember that resilience is based

on communal activity and mutual support. Use available services, engage with your community, and approach the healing process with commitment and optimism.

Chapter 10: Restoring Essential Services and Utilities—Reconnecting to the Necessities of Life

Disasters often interrupt the fabric of our everyday lives, cutting off access to critical services and utilities such as clean water, sanitation, food, and communication. In the aftermath, restoring these lifelines is critical to safeguarding public health and well-being while also aiding the entire recovery process. This chapter looks into practical ways for managing this critical period, helping you to reclaim control and restore routine following trauma.

Safe Water Treatment and Sanitation Practices: Quenching Thirst while Protecting Health
Access to clean water and good sanitation are critical for avoiding disease outbreaks and protecting health during and after catastrophes.

Water treatment:
Boiling: Heating water to a rolling boil for at least one minute successfully destroys the

majority of dangerous bacteria and parasites. This is still the easiest and most dependable way in many cases.

Chemical Disinfection: To disinfect clear water, use chlorine tablets or iodine solutions. To guarantee efficient disinfection, carefully follow the manufacturer's recommendations and use the right amount.

Filtration: Portable water filters may remove debris and some toxins from mildly turbid water. Choose filters that are approved for certain pollutants depending on the hazards in your location.

Solar Disinfection: Filling transparent plastic bottles with polluted water and exposing them to direct sunshine for at least six hours may be an efficient disinfection approach in areas with plenty of sunlight.

Always choose safe water sources over possibly polluted ones. If you're doubtful about the safety of a water source, treat it before drinking.

Sanitation:
Latrines and sanitation facilities: If current facilities are destroyed or unavailable, use

available materials to build temporary latrines that guarantee correct human waste disposal and avoid contamination. Follow safe latrine building requirements to reduce environmental impact and health concerns.

Handwashing: Regular handwashing with soap and clean water is essential for avoiding illness transmission. If soap is unavailable, try using ash or dirt mixed with water as a temporary substitute.

Hygiene Practices: Maintain personal hygiene, wash clothing on a regular basis, and keep living areas clean to reduce the risk of infection and disease outbreaks.

Prioritizing water treatment and good sanitation procedures protects public health and creates the groundwork for a successful recovery process. Collaborate with your community to create sanitation facilities and encourage hygienic habits to guarantee everyone's well-being.

Food Safety and Hygiene During Recovery: Feeding Bodies and Preventing Illness

After a tragedy, it is even more important to have safe and nutritional meals. Following basic food safety and hygiene standards during recovery guarantees critical nutrients while reducing the danger of foodborne infections.

Food storage and handling:
To minimize food deterioration, prioritize fresh and perishable goods. Maintain temperature control to prevent bacterial development. If refrigeration is not available, use ice-filled coolers or alternate chilling techniques. Properly store dry foods in airtight containers to prevent moisture, insects, and contamination. Maintain hygiene throughout food preparation. Before and after handling food, wash your hands thoroughly with soap and water, and make sure your utensils and cooking surfaces are clean.

If you are doubtful about the safety of a food, toss it. Avoid eating anything that seems rotten, discolored, or has an unpleasant odor.

Nutrition and Food Sourcing:

Focus on nutrient-rich foods: Prioritize consuming foods rich in proteins, carbohydrates, vitamins, and minerals to maintain energy levels and support the body's recovery processes.

Community gardens and food sharing: Collaborate with your community to establish temporary gardens or utilize food sharing networks to supplement available food sources.

Nutritional support programs: Seek out government or humanitarian aid programs that provide emergen

Access to healthy food is critical for physical and mental health throughout rehabilitation. Prioritize food safety and cleanliness measures, look into alternate food sources, and take use of available assistance programs to ensure your nutritional requirements are satisfied.

Using Alternative Power Sources and Communication Channels to Reconnect and Restore Services

Disruptions to electricity and communication networks may impede recovery efforts and isolate populations. Exploring different options may close the distance and enable reconnection:

Alternative power sources:
Solar panels: Portable solar panels and rechargeable batteries may provide electricity for lights, communication devices, and small appliances. Consider investing in these long-term catastrophe preparation options.
Generators: Portable generators may power bigger appliances and equipment, but they must be properly ventilated and operated safely to prevent carbon monoxide poisoning.
Community Power Hubs: Collaborate with your community to set up temporary power hubs powered by generators or other alternative sources, allowing everyone to share access to energy for basic necessities.

Ham radio: Ham radio operators play a crucial role in emergency communication during disasters, providing a reliable means of communication beyond disrupted networks. Consider acquiring a license and basic training to contribute to community communication efforts. Community message boards: Establish physical or online community message boards to share information, coordinate activities, and locate missing individuals. Satellite phones: For critical needs in remote areas, satellite phones offer communication even when terrestrial networks are down.

Signal boosting and mesh networks: Consider using community initiatives and technology to boost existing weak signals or create temporary mesh networks for wider communication reach.

Ingenuity and collaboration are key in restoring communication channels. Explore available options, utilize technology responsibly, and contribute to community efforts to rebuild your communication infrastructure. Beyond the Basics: Leveraging Technology for Efficient Restoration and Communication

Advances in technology offer tools and platforms that can enhance the restoration process and communication efforts: Drone technology: Drones can be used to assess damage to infrastructure, map affected areas, and facilitate targeted repair efforts. Mobile applications: Several disaster response apps provide information on shelters, resources, safety tips, and communication channels, empowering individuals to navigate the recovery process effectively.

Social media platforms: Utilize social media platforms for information sharing, connecting with support networks, and coordinating community activities during recovery. Responsible and strategic use of technology can significantly amplify recovery efforts and communication reach. Stay informed about available tools, utilize them ethically, and contribute to building a more resilient and technologically empowered community.

Case Studies in Effective Service Restoration and Communication:

The swift repair of electrical grids and communication networks after Hurricane Sandy in 2012, where collaboration between utility companies, government agencies, and communities facilitated rapid restoration of essential services.

The innovative use of drones and satellite imagery to assess damage and coordinate relief efforts in the aftermath of the Nepal earthquake in 2015, contributing to a more targeted and efficient recovery process. * The community-driven establishment of temporary radio networks and message boards after the wildfires in California in 2018, ensuring information flow and facilitating coordination among displaced individuals and response teams. These examples showcase the importance of collaboration, utilizing technology, and adopting innovative approaches to restore essential services and communication channels during the recovery phase. By learning from successful strategies and adapting them to your context, you can contribute to building a more resilient and adaptable community in the face of future challenges.

National and local public health and utility service providers

Moving Forward: Towards a Reconnected and Resilient Future. Restoring essential services and communication channels is a cornerstone of the recovery process. By prioritizing safe water, food, hygiene, and reconnecting with information and support networks, communities can rebuild their infrastructure, regain a sense of normalcy, and pave the way for a more resilient future.

Collaboration, resourcefulness, and the utilization of available technology are crucial assets in navigating this critical phase. Embrace the collective spirit, share your knowledge and skills, and contribute to building a community that is prepared to face future challenges with strength and resilience

Chapter 11: Rebuilding Your Home and Community—Rising from the Rubble with Determination and Unity

The aftermath of a catastrophe causes not only physical devastation, but also an emotional burden of dislocation and uncertainty. Rebuilding your house and neighborhood is an important stage in the recovery process, as it restores normality and fosters hope for the future. This chapter digs into managing this period, allowing you to rebuild your house, handle financial losses, and embrace the power of community support on your road to a better future.

Repairing Structural Damage: Brick by Brick Rebuilding Your Sanctuary
Assessing and fixing structural damage in your house requires a controlled approach that emphasizes safety and follows correct criteria.

Safety First:

Do not enter a structurally challenged structure: If your house seems unstable, with obvious cracks, collapsed walls, or broken foundations, stay away and notify emergency services or building inspectors for a safety assessment.

When assessing damage, wear protective clothing, gloves, and masks to avoid debris, dust, and potential hazards. If safe, turn off gas, electricity, and water supplies before entering the building to prevent further damage or safety risks.

Professional assessment and repair:

Consult licensed contractors, engineers, and architects for damage assessment and recommendations for repair or reconstruction.

Obtain permits and approvals from local authorities before starting any major repairs or reconstruction work.

Follow all applicable building codes and safety regulations.

Always prioritize safety throughout the repair procedure. Do not be afraid to seek expert assistance from trained professionals to assure the quality and stability of your home's reconstruction.

Beyond the Basics: Sustainable Approaches to Reconstruction
Consider using sustainable and resilient strategies in your rehabilitation efforts.

Eco-friendly materials: Choose ecologically friendly construction materials such as recycled content timber, energy-efficient windows, and sustainable insulation to lessen your environmental effect and produce a more energy-efficient home.
Disaster-resistant features: Consider reinforced roofs, wind-resistant windows, and flood-resistant foundations to improve your home's resilience against future disasters.
Community-based initiatives: Partner with your community to explore sustainable rebuilding practices and resource sharing to reduce environmental impact and create a more resilient neighborhood.

Managing Financial Losses and Claims: Reducing the Economic Burden
Financial losses after a calamity may be daunting. Understanding insurance coverage and various support programs may reduce the economic strain and aid a speedier recovery.

Insurance Claim:
Review your policy: Understand your insurance policy's terms and coverage details to understand what losses are covered and the claims process. Document losses: Gather thorough documentation of the damage, including photographs, videos, receipts, and repair estimates to support your insurance claim. File your claim promptly: Contact your insurance company as soon as possible to initiate the claims process and avoid potential delays.

Governmental Assistance Programs:
Disaster relief grants: Investigate government programs offering financial assistance for repairs, temporary housing, and other essential needs in the aftermath of a disaster.

Low-interest loans: Investigate loan programs with subsidized interest rates specifically designed to assist individuals and communities affected by disasters. Tax relief measures: Look for tax deductions or credits offered by the government to help offset financial losses incurred due

Use available resources to overcome the financial constraints of rebuilding. Seek professional help if required, and fight for your rights to obtain fair compensation and access to critical resources.

Community Support and Resilience: Rise Together, Stronger Than Ever
A community's strength comes from its collective spirit and readiness to help one another in times of need. Embracing community support and promoting resilience are critical components in restoring your house and neighborhood:

Volunteerism and Mutual Aid:

Volunteer your time and skills: Help others by cleaning debris, preparing meals, providing childcare, or offering emotional support.

Organize aid networks: Create or join community aid networks to share resources, coordinate volunteer efforts, and ensure everyone's needs are met. Donate resources: If you have extra resources, consider donating food, clothing, building materials, or financial contributions

Promoting Mental and Emotional Wellbeing:

Organize support groups: Start or join support groups to connect with others who have had similar experiences, exchange coping techniques, and provide emotional support to one another.

Seek professional help: Do not be afraid to seek professional mental health care if you are experiencing difficulties such as anxiety, depression, or trauma in the aftermath of the accident. Trained therapists can provide helpful tools and methods for dealing with emotional upheaval and navigating the healing process.

Prioritize self-care: Do things that improve your personal well-being, such as frequent exercise, good diet, and sticking to a consistent sleep pattern. These techniques help to build emotional resilience and improve your capacity to handle obstacles and assist others.

Celebrate Milestones and Foster Hope:
Commemorate little victories: Recognize and celebrate even minor accomplishments throughout the rebuilding process, no matter how trivial they seem. This raises morale, promotes the perception of progress, and maintains optimism.
Organize community activities: Plan and attend community events that promote connection, celebrate togetherness, and allow for shared pleasure and laughter. These meetings may help to promote healing, develop social relationships, and restore hope for the future.
Embrace the spirit of resilience: Recognize that communities have overcome enormous problems throughout history. Draw inspiration from previous resilience tales and your community's collective spirit to fuel your own

drive and help establish a stronger, more unified future.

Case Studies for Successful Community Rebuilding:
In Aceh, Indonesia, communities used participatory ways to rebuild houses and infrastructure with disaster-resilient elements after the tsunami. Following Hurricane Katrina, New Orleans' recovery relied on grassroots initiatives, volunteer work, and creative architectural ideas to recreate thriving neighborhoods and develop resilience. The collective reaction to California's wildfires, in which communities banded together to set up temporary shelters, give emotional support, and restore destroyed towns, demonstrated the strength of unity and teamwork in the face of tragedy.

These instances demonstrate the necessity of community support, teamwork, and resilience throughout the rebuilding process. By learning from successful recovery efforts, tailoring solutions to your individual situation, and embracing the spirit of togetherness, you may help to develop a stronger, more resilient community that flourishes in the face of future adversity.

Moving Forward: Building a Future Founded on Strength and Solidarity
Rebuilding your house and neighborhood requires perseverance, effort, and shared optimism. You may traverse this time with bravery and purpose by putting safety first, efficiently managing financial obstacles, and embracing the power of community support.

Every contribution, act of kindness, and collaborative effort feeds the collective spirit of resilience, paving the road for a better, stronger future. As you rebuild your house, brick by brick, you are also helping to rebuild a community that will be remembered for the resilience and togetherness it found in the face of hardship.

Chapter 12: Lessons Learned and Continuous Improvement—Preparing for an Uncertain Future with Wisdom and Growth

While the aftermath of a tragedy creates obstacles, it also provides important chances for development. Reflecting on your experiences, assessing your reaction, and changing your plans can help you and your community handle future uncertainty with better resilience and readiness. This chapter digs into the critical process of continuous improvement, instructing you on how to use lessons gained to better your personal and collective preparation for the changing risk environment.

Evaluating Your Preparedness and Response: A Retrospective for Improved Preparedness
Examining your readiness and reaction to the recent crisis helps you to discover areas for

improvement, strengthen current plans, and build on your strengths.

Strengths and Achievements:
Identify what worked well: Consider which components of your preparation and reaction were beneficial. Was your emergency kit sufficient? Did your communication strategy encourage information sharing? Recognizing your talents boosts confidence and serves as a basis for future tactics.
Acknowledge individual and communal efforts: Recognize the contributions of yourself, your family, and your community in overcoming obstacles. Recognizing joint talents promotes unity and encourages ongoing cooperation.

Weaknesses and gaps:
Analyze areas for improvement: Be honest about where your preparation fell short. Did you lack any particular supplies? Did the communication channels fail? Identifying flaws enables you to remedy them and avoid similar vulnerabilities in the future.
Collect input from others: Request constructive input from family, neighbors, and community

members. Their viewpoints may reveal blind spots and provide significant recommendations for change.

Evaluating your preparation does not include self-criticism, but rather positive introspection and improvement. Adopt a learning mentality, concentrate on discovering areas for growth, and recognize the useful lessons learned from your experiences.

Updating and Refining Your Plans and Supplies: Adapting to a Changing Risk Environment.
The nature of catastrophes and threats might change with time. Regularly revising your plans and supplies guarantees that you are prepared for a shifting terrain.

Adapting to new risks:
Analyze emerging threats. Stay updated on new or changing dangers in your area, such as greater flood risk from climate change or cyber security threats. Adjust your preparation plans and supplies to reflect these new concerns.

Stay current with local guidelines: Review and update your preparations to reflect any changes to local emergency response methods or evacuation procedures.

Incorporating Lesson Learned:
Revise your emergency plan: Based on your review, make changes to your emergency plan to address any shortcomings that were found. Update contact information, evacuation routes, communication techniques, and any special needs concerns.

Upgrade your emergency kit. Improve your emergency pack depending on the holes you've noticed. Include extra supplies depending on individual requirements or lessons gained, ensuring that it addresses your specific weaknesses and circumstances.

Preparedness is a continuous process, not a single event. Regularly review your plans and supplies, adapting them to changing threats and your personal experiences to ensure they stay relevant and successful in the face of unexpected circumstances.

Sharing Knowledge and Educating Others: Establishing a Preparedness Culture in Your Community
Sharing your experiences and thoughts may have a ripple effect, building a culture of preparation in your community.

Personal Outreach:
Please share your story: Inform friends, family, and neighbors about your experiences. Discuss what worked well, what problems you encountered, and what you learnt. Your personal narrative has the potential to connect with others and motivate them to take preparation seriously.
Plan preparation workshops: Share your knowledge and experience by leading courses on disaster preparation principles, particular dangers in your region, or subjects such as emergency kit construction and first aid techniques.

Community initiatives:
Promote community preparation programs: Urge local governments and groups to invest in community-wide preparedness activities such

as hazard awareness campaigns, public exercises, and training programs.

Collaborate with local groups: Work with schools, community centers, and faith-based organizations to raise awareness about disaster preparation and inspire group action.

By sharing your knowledge and actively contributing to the development of a preparation culture in your community, you are empowering others to face future problems with more confidence and resilience.

Case Studies for Continuous Improvement and Community Preparedness:

The Sendai Framework for Disaster Risk Reduction is a worldwide roadmap for boosting international collaboration and strengthening local disaster preparation and risk reduction capabilities, with a focus on continuous improvement and information exchange.

Community-based early warning systems in Asian coastal communities combine traditional knowledge and contemporary technology to forecast and react to tsunamis, demonstrating the value of local efforts and information sharing. Neighborhood preparation networks are being established in numerous places throughout the globe, where citizens pool resources, skills, and knowledge to develop collective resilience and a culture of mutual assistance in the case of catastrophe.

These examples emphasize the value of ongoing development, responding to changing risks, and sharing information throughout communities. By learning from successful programs and adapting them to your particular situation, you may help to develop a more resilient and prepared society.

Moving Forward: Cultivating a Growth Mindset for a Resilient Future

The path to readiness is an ongoing cycle of learning, adjusting, and evolving. By adopting a growth mindset, reflecting on your experiences, and actively contributing to the development of a preparation culture in your community, you become a resilient agent, enabling yourself and others to confront future uncertainty with confidence and strength. Remember that even modest efforts toward readiness may make a big impact, and by working together, we can create a world where communities are ready to tackle difficulties, recover from hardship, and prosper in the aftermath of any crisis.

Further Exploration
This chapter establishes a framework for ongoing development and community preparation. To go further into certain elements, consider examining the following:

Risk-specific preparation: Investigate unique threats in your region, such as earthquakes, floods, or wildfires, and customize your preparedness plans and supplies appropriately.
Psychological preparedness: Learn how to cope with stress, anxiety, and trauma during and after disasters to build emotional resilience.
Vulnerability assessment: Evaluate your home and community to identify areas at risk and implement mitigation strategies to minimize potential damage.
Technological tools for preparedness: Investigate apps, online platforms, and communication technologies.

By actively participating in these areas of exploration, you may continue to improve your readiness, contribute to a more resilient community, and pave the path for a future in which we tackle problems together, armed with information, cooperation, and an unyielding spirit of resilience.

Made in United States
Troutdale, OR
09/12/2024